AF266942

# *Abraham, Isaac,*
# *and the Altar of Fire*

*Did God foretell the future sacrifice
of his own son?*

*God Bless You*

## Joe S. Amer-I-Can

**To order additional copies of this book, contact:**
*Proisle Publishing Services LLC*
*39-67 58th 1st Floor Woodside*
*New York, NY 11377, USA*
*Phone: (+1 347-922-3779)*
*info@proislepublishing.com*

# DEDICATION

This book is dedicated to God, family, community, our military, and the over 1.4 million Amer-I can soldiers who have given their lives and the millions more who have been wounded so we can choose freedom over dependence. Their surviving family members were broken so ours could remain whole. The vast majority of our nation's heroes were Christian. They fought, died, and came home maimed in mind and limb, but they did not give in to the same types of tyranny America has been fighting since the miraculous birth of our nation. During the 5,000 years before we were founded, tyranny in all its forms was the bully which made sheep out of ordinary men and women. Because of America, the bully was vanquished, so we can all work hard to make our dreams come true, no matter how great the dreams are.

# AMER-I CAN PRAYER

No ordinary souls our fighters
When on their knees they prayed

Five thousand years of tyranny
Proclaims all tyrants slain

Dear God, please forgive us
And grant this one request

Keep off the cloak of tyranny
And put us to Thy test.

Of faith, and hope, and love
In keeping with your son

For these great gifts, we pledge
Our Joyful Revolution!

# Abraham, Isaac
# & the Altar of Fire

No one loved playing "Challenge" more than Isaac. It was a game he and his young friends created to entertain themselves when the desert sun started to fall in the western sky. They could hardly wait for the heat of the day to subside and it becomes cool enough for them to convert their shepherd's staff into the special clubs they modified to play the game. Isaac and a few of the other boys went so far as to make a second club, dedicated more to "Challenge" than shepherding. He called his club Lightning and proudly carved the name into its handle.

It was a simple game born from the barren surroundings of the desert: first, either by chance or by choice, they divided themselves into equally numbered teams. (Lately, the boys had become two teams: the Raiders and the Hornets.) Then a field was marked off in the sand and dirt. It was about one hundred cubits wide (50 yards) and about two hundred cubits long (100 yards). A ten-foot-by-four-foot goal was lined off in the center of both ends. To their dismay, every time they established a good playing ground, the grownups would come along for one reason or another and make them move it.

From the hardest wood the boys could find, they carved rough-looking balls and then begged one of their mothers to stitch leather (from goat hide) around them. When sewn properly, the ball would fly off their curved-nosed staffs. Isaac had several of these balls—some to practice with and a few just for important games. Next to the beautiful coat, his mother made him, they were his most prized possessions.

Each goal was tended by a goalie. The rest of the team passed the ball from club to club until such time as a shot on goal was attempted. One point for each goal scored, and three points for a successful challenge, which could be called for at any time by any player brash or courageous enough to attempt to carry it out. A challenge meant team play was stopped long enough for a lone player to take his club and the ball and challenge the opposing team's goalie. Within a designated area about forty cubits from the goal, the challenger could fake and taunt the goalie as much as he wanted before finally taking the shot that he prayed would cross the goal line.

Challenge attempts, except toward the end of the game when one team was behind by a large margin, were rare. If the score was close, the consequences for failing to score on a challenge attempt were just too severe to try random loners. If a player called for a challenge on his own, without consulting his team, and then failed to score it, his teammates would scrum around him and give him a group pummeling that was proportionate to his failure. Depending on the circumstances, these punishments could be good-natured and even funny—often ending with the whole team down on the ground laughing and hilariously screaming. But they could also be used to mete out real punishment—sometimes to settle old feuds, which may not have anything to do with the game. Many scars and an occasional broken bone told the stories on the bodies of those who dared challenge at the wrong time and fail.

There were no referees in "Challenge"—no adult to stand between an individual infraction and the final judgment of the group. There was nothing except the popularity of Isaac, who was becoming as revered by the young people as his father, Abraham, was by the older generation.

He was his father's and his mother's son, promised to them in their later years by God. Abraham was a well-seasoned one-hundred-year-old, while Sarah, at ninety, finally gave birth to her only child. It all came about just as the Lord had promised. He told them to call him Isaac, which in Hebrew means, "He laughs." After Isaac was born, Sarah told everyone, "God has brought me laughter (joy), and everyone who hears about this will laugh with me."

But good-natured Isaac didn't always laugh. He, like all the kids, also suffered under the bullying of Tubal, who knew just how to do it without getting caught by the adults. Tubal's evil ways came upon him gradually, in equal measure with his enormous size. He welcomed them with vigor, even glee. At first the other kids were drawn to his jaunty power. He was the captain of the Raiders, while Isaac headed the Hornets. Tubal was nearing adulthood, with a budding dark beard, plenty of body hair, and a deep voice to match. He was also a huge freak of nature with a massive frame and limbs that were frightening for everyone to behold, especially the younger kids. To add to his enormous evil continence, Tubal had sinister, penetrating eyes, with the right one angling from the center, giving him a menacing look that underscored the rumor that he descended from Cain.

By tribal custom, he should have already moved on to the adult grouping, where rumor said he intimidated some of the older men so he could stay with the young people. The adults of Abraham's tribe didn't want to be around Tubal either. As young as he was, he was beginning to have visions of power that would one day see him attempt to divide the thousands who followed Abraham.

The bully knew he could count on Isaac's sense of pride to keep him safe. Isaac would have taken a beating before he would let anyone know that Tubal was making his life miserable. For some reason, all his own, Abraham's heir wouldn't use his high position in the tribe to bring the wrath of the tribal council down on his tormenter, let alone go to his father, who might deal the ultimate punishment to Tubal. One sharp command from Father Abraham and he would be forced to roam the desert alone until he met a terrifying end to his life.

The older, larger Tubal hated everything about Isaac, from his natural good looks and pleasant disposition to the obvious love and respect Isaac had for his aging parents. But most of all, he detested the fact that as Isaac was growing older, the younger boys, and some of the older ones, were gravitating toward him. It was becoming increasingly obvious they enjoyed being around Isaac for all the right reasons. Just as obvious was the fact that before long the bully would begin to lose his leadership position, one he and his followers had been holding together with cruelty and intimidation for several years. Because of Isaac's popularity, the situation was becoming desperate for Tubal.

As usual, Isaac and his friends were spending their day near the foothills tending their flocks of goats and sheep. They were far from their settlement and the eyes of the adult tribe members. Because they had been occurring for many seasons, they had almost grown accustomed to the periodic attacks of Tubal and his small gang. Today, they were too busy planning their next "Challenge" strategy and testing a new shot one of them was showing the group to notice any signs of a pending strike.

"Look out, Isaac!"

The scream came from Enosh, Isaac's best friend. It was just in time to give him the fraction of a second he needed to dodge a huge bolder, which came bounding through their midst. Suddenly, Tubal and his gang were upon them. Cursing and screaming, they threw stones and shoved several boys to the ground. Their plan was not to stand and fight but to frighten with the boulder and then cause as much panic and fear as they could by running through the group and appearing on the other side. Their screams and the dust had barely subsided when Tubal shouted, "Curses on you, Isaac, and your little band of desert lice! We will crush all of you in the next "Challenge" match!"

With that warning, they disappeared into the desert, leaving a few of Isaac's younger friends in tears and the rest of them trying to catch their breath. Isaac was shaken also, but he did not panic. Something inside him told him to stay calm and assess the situation. He remembered his father's admonition to always trust the Lord in good times and in bad.

"What are we going to do now?" cried Seth, the youngest of the young, as he wiped away his tears. "'Old One Eye' is going to put together a 'Challenge' team that will destroy us! I'm not going back to the camp until he is a toothless old man, so weak he can't even fart."

The boys had to laugh, and with their laughter, the spell of fear was broken.

Isaac took command. "Easy does it, my friends. Let's not give wicked 'Oneball' any more credit than he deserves. Just because he can pry a boulder loose with his staff doesn't mean he knows how to beat us at 'Challenge' with it. It doesn't take a whole lot of anything to pull a trick like the one he just pulled. Besides, we've nearly beaten them before. What makes you think we can't finally do it?"

Little Seth came back with, "But, Isaac, it's easy for you to talk. You're the son of Abraham, and you've grown nearly a foot in the last year. What about we little ones? How can we play against Tubal's bullies?"

"You have to believe," Isaac said. "All of us must remember our prayers from now on and trust in the Lord that he will deliver us from Tubal's bullying. He will help us if we put forth our best effort and don't give up until the day is won. Let's get back to our planning session and that new shot Kenan was showing us."

This time Isaac posted a lookout before the group began to practice the new shot. By accident, the observant Kenan had discovered that he could make the ball curve. He took his club and began to demonstrate.

"If I put my hands together on my staff like this, as in prayer, and then turn them to the right a little bit and point my feet and shoulders to the right also, I feel like I'm swinging more from the inside, and the ball curves in the air from right to left. It's amazing! And if I do the opposite—turn my hands to the left on the grip, open my feet and shoulders to the left, while swinging more from out to in—the ball curves from left to right."

Kenan was prone to exaggeration, so the boys were naturally skeptical of his new discovery. They were used to seeing the ball curve, which was the nature of things. But to have the ability to curve the ball at will was more than they could believe without demonstration. Now that they were seeing Kenan perform this magic before their eyes, they were amazed and so excited that the previous attack slipped from their minds. The boys took turns trying to make the ball turn in the air. Of course, the younger boys struggled the most with the new shot. They all chuckled when little Seth fell to the ground trying to swing too hard. He was so small a strong wind could blow him away.

When Isaac finally took his turn, all eyes were upon him. He was a natural athlete who loved to learn new moves and methods. Having seen all the attempts before him, he felt confident he could make the ball curve. The way he placed his hands on Ole Lighting and the way he moved into the shot told everyone Abraham and Sarah's son was blessed with all the confidence in the world.

"Do you see that large rock over there?" Isaac pointed as he spoke. "I'm going to try and curve the ball around to the right of it and then back to the bushes on the far left."

None of the boys doubted what they were about to see, because they had seen Isaac do things like this many times before. It was almost as if the boys helped will it to happen and all that was left to do was watch it unfold.

Isaac stepped up to the ball, played it back in his stance a little more than anyone else had, and then made a beautiful, effortless swing that seemed to flow on forever. The ball shot straight forward on a line for the right side of the rock and then curved to the left, landing in the exact middle of the bushes he had pointed to earlier! The boys let out a cheer just as the feat was accomplished, which built on the admiration and respect they felt for Isaac.

Isaac turned toward his friends, smiled, and said, "It's all timing, boys," as if everyone possessed the same magical rhythm he did.

# THE SECRET JOURNEY

That evening Isaac had a difficult time falling asleep. His mind was swimming with the events of the day: his near miss with the boulder; Tubal's curse; the upcoming "Challenge" match; and the thrill of learning a new shot, which he knew would figure large in his team's offense. How could they possibly win a match against the feared Raiders? On average, the bullies were older, bigger, and stronger and played much dirtier. Isaac knew they had come close before in less serious matches. But he also knew the evil giant would stop at nothing to win, especially now that he had issued his dreaded curse. Tubal would have to follow through with his smashing threat or face the end of his reign of terror. It was late, but the worried Isaac could not find rest.

He was still wide awake when he heard his father's entourage approach their leader's tent, staked out right next to his. He heard Abraham issue orders to the twins, Jabal and Jubal, his most trusted servants whose incredible loyalty was as interchangeable between them as their stoic dispositions.

Abraham spoke. "Listen to me carefully. Tomorrow, we will leave for the region of Moriah, about three days' journey. Yahweh has spoken to me and told me to go there and make a burnt offering to him. I will chop the wood for the offering myself in the morning. You two will gather it, pack the donkeys for the journey, and be prepared to leave as soon as possible. I am taking Isaac with me."

They answered in unison, "Yes, Master."

At the sound of his name, Isaac bolted straight up from his bedding. All in the camp, which spread for a mile in each direction, were accustomed to doing the bidding of their leader. Many thousands tuned to the commands of one man. But this was very unusual; never before had Isaac traveled in this fashion with his famous father. Instead of a tribe of thousands, they would be accompanied by only two servants, Jabal and Jubal, so loyal to Abraham and his family that they would faithfully die for them.

Now Isaac's curiosity was piqued even further. He had to know more. After he heard his father enter his parent's tent, he snuck out of his own quarters, crept past the guards, and listened with his ear against their tent. He heard Abraham repeat to his wife almost the same thing he told his two servants, this time with a definite tone of sadness in his voice.

He said, "I leave at dawn for Moriah. I will take Isaac with me."

Sarah cried, "Why must you take Isaac with you? He is still too young to make such a dangerous journey into the mountains. Surely you can do the Lord's bidding and make your burnt sacrifice without Isaac having to travel all that way. We have waited all these many years for God to bless us with Isaac. What will we do if something should happen to him in the dangerous mountains?"

Abraham paused for a moment, wondering whether to tell Sarah that Yahweh was asking for more than just any burnt offering. He was asking for the return of Isaac's soul to him. He decided it would be too much for her heart to bear.

"Sarah, as always, we must do as the Lord asks. You know that he has blessed our nation for many generations because we live righteously in his

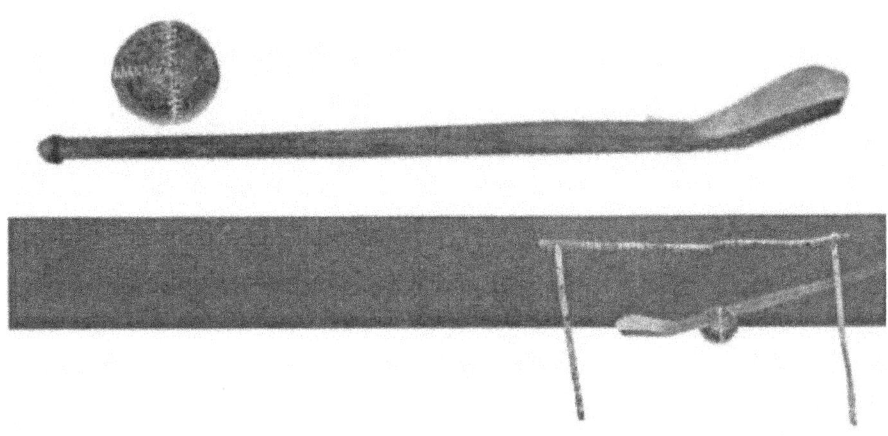

name. He has commanded me to bring Isaac with me to Moriah; therefore, I must!"

Sarah could not argue with Abraham's reasoning. Their young community had indeed been blessed, multiplying into a nation of many thousands while surmounting the difficulties that had befallen them since they left Haran, the land of their forefathers and the place Yahweh had commanded them to leave. God told Abraham he would bless him and his followers if he did so.

Sarah's heart was heavy, but she knew Abraham was once again doing the right thing by loving and serving the Lord. And yet she was seized with a deep sense of foreboding about her husband and her young son's mysterious journey.

Isaac crept back into his tent. Now he was troubled even more. After lying there for some time, trying to figure everything out, he decided he was powerless against many of the problems that were facing him. Could he lead his team against the dark powers of Tubal and save his young friends from a sound beating, and who knows how many more years of bullying? And even more disturbing if that's possible, why was his father taking him so far into the mountains against his mother's wishes? There was something very troubling about the tone of her voice as she pleaded against the idea of him going to Moriah with his father.

Tossing and turning in his tent, Isaac couldn't remember being more afraid of the future. His normal confidence was draining from his spirit like the desert sun draining moisture from his body. He cried out in despair.

In an instant, two guards were peering inside his tent. One of them asked, "Are you all right, young master? We heard a cry! Shall we wake your father?"

Coming to his senses, Isaac answered, "No. I am fine, only a bad dream. Forgive my outcry, please."

Once the guards returned to their posts, Isaac started to calm down. The mere mentioning of his father, whom he loved second only to the Lord, had a peaceful effect on him. He felt the same way about his mother. It was just that he had never known of a quarrel between his parents, especially one involving him. He remembered a prayer they often shared together:

*Oh Lord, we love, honor, and adore you. Please guide our family in your ways and be with us throughout our lives together. We thank you, Lord, for your blessings upon us. We know you are with us always.*

Isaac repeated it over and over: "We know you are with us always. We know you are with us always ..." He was soon fast asleep.

The next morning, Abraham excused Isaac from his shepherding duties so he could help him cut the firewood that he would use to sacrifice

his own son. The supreme irony of the chore was not lost on Abraham, but he felt he needed this time with Isaac before they would leave later that day. Over the many decades of his life, Abraham lived by one unbending principle: to love, trust, and serve the Lord. He punctuated this principle and made it his own by always doing the Lord's bidding promptly, exactly, and without question.

God's words still resounded in his head, "Abraham!"

"Here I am," he replied.

Then God said, "Take your son, your only son, Isaac, whom you love, and go to the region of Moriah. Sacrifice him there as a burnt offering on one of the mountains I will tell you about."

No instruction could have been clearer or more horrifying!

He felt that God had chosen him as the leader of his people because he possessed certain traits. They were required of him if his people were to survive their journeys in the desert and all that was demanded of them in their harsh environment. Yahweh had tested his faith many times, but none more than the time he told him to gather his faithful people around him and leave Haran, their homeland, for the unknown desert. Abraham gave the order to do so immediately.

While a few in his tribe had questioned his leadership, most followed him as he followed the Lord, which was much more difficult for them. Could he expect them to follow him and do his bidding without question if he was not just as willing to do the same for the Lord? He knew if he wavered for just one moment, all the doubt in the world would creep in, and those among his people who were weak would seize that moment to turn the rest of his people against him. He knew in his heart of hearts that if he did what Yahweh told him without hesitation, the rest would be in the Lord's hands, a very safe place to be indeed.

Abraham had followed this pattern so many times; it was second nature to him. Except this time was different in many ways; this time he wouldn't be able to busy himself preparing thousands of people to mobilize on some great adventure, no war to fight, no army to lead. This time he would have three lonely days in the company of his loving and adoring son to contemplate the vilest mission any father could ever imagine.

Abraham's musings while chopping wood was interrupted by Isaac's question. "Father, why will we leave our home and travel so far into the mountains? What awaits us there in Moriah?"

"Because Yahweh has commanded it, my son. And the only thing we can be sure of is that he will guide us. We must trust and serve the Lord."

Isaac knew his father so well. The questions were more to break their silence than provide any definitive answer, or were they? Upon reflection, maybe that was all anyone really needed to know about anything. Do the best you can in life. After that, you must love and trust the Lord—how simple, how complicated all in one. *But if we choose to follow the Lord, he lifts the veil of complication and reveals himself to us.*

Isaac whispered to himself, "Trust the Lord." He was comforted by his father's words, his own inner strength, and the presence of Yahweh inside him.

As always, they timed their departure for mid-afternoon so the setting sun would provide them the relief they needed to accomplish the initial part of their journey. No man or beast traveled very far in the desert when the sun was near vertical in the sky. Sarah followed them to the outlines of their settlement and watched as their figures disappeared into the horizon and the looming mountains. Her fears and her prayers went with them.

After reflecting on what Abraham had told her about God's command, she knew their lives and the lives of her entire nation would be forever affected by what would come out of this journey. Even so, her mother's heart was still heavy with fear and apprehension for Isaac.

Isaac shifted his weight on his donkey once again. All in the little group were appreciative of the wonderful beasts. Their steadfast and sure-footed ways would be tested severely in the mountains looming just ahead. The young boy had traveled great distances with his nation, but always after lengthy encampments, and never over the mountains. All the stories he had heard about them spoke of great fear and danger, like huge mountain cats, snakes, scorpions, and spiders the size of a man's hand, not to mention precipitous drops from heights that take your breath away! With all the time in the world to think and worry, he decided to take his clue on how to handle the trip from his four-footed friends—one measured step at a time. He would try not to let his mind race ahead to any pitfalls that might be waiting for him.

The setting sun reminded him he would miss several days of "Challenge" practice with his friends. At this very moment, they would be warming up. He saw them in his mind's eye. He could almost hear the excitement in their voices as they readied themselves for a mock game. His good friend, Enosh, would be leading them onto the makeshift practice field.

He had spoken to his lieutenant about the need to keep the team focused—even going so far as to tell him to be as rough as possible with them in preparation for the big match. He shared his father's philosophy with him that the legs feed the wolf. They must be strong indeed if the younger, smaller team is to stay in the big match. With the proper preparation, he knew his young team would play bravely and not back down. When he closed his eyes for a moment, he could almost see and hear them laughing and shouting at each other. From many miles away, he still felt like he was with them. He was glad that Enosh was a good leader who would not allow the rest of the team to slack off in any way.

They camped that night in the higher foothills. They had made good time and were in an excellent position from which to make the ascent into the mountains the next morning. Isaac helped Jabal and Jubal make camp, while Abraham busied himself with the evening's fire. Like all great leaders, Abraham never asked anyone to do something he wouldn't do

himself. There was little talk, as everyone in the party knew their role. There was a tent for the two servants and one for father and son.

Isaac went off by himself and practiced the new shot. This would be the last day of the trip that the terrain would allow such practice. The more he worked at it, the better he got, until he discovered he could curve the ball great distances.

When Isaac got back to camp, Abraham led the four of them in evening prayers. He asked Isaac to make the final entreaty to Yahweh before they all entered their respective tents.

"And what do you ask of our Lord this evening, my son?"

The young lad was more than a little nervous, praying before his great father on earth, the greater Father in heaven, and the two trusted servants, whose humble ways humbled him in return. Then he remembered how his nerves were calmed the night before and said, "Father, if it's all right with you, I would like to include Jabal and Jubal in our family prayer tonight and our donkeys also."

"Of course, my brave son," came his father's loving reply.

Then Isaac recited from memory, "Oh Lord, we love, honor, and adore you. Please guide our family in your ways, and be with us throughout our lives together. We thank you, Lord, for your blessings upon us. We know you are with us always."

The family prayer reminded him of his mother, so he added, "And please be close to mother these days we are gone. We know she worries terribly about us. Amen."

"Amen," they all answered and then entered their tents.

Isaac's prayer was all Abraham could take. He choked back his emotions while he was saying it, for fear he would reveal the real purpose of their trip. It was all he could do to keep from crying out in anguish! He loved Sarah and Isaac in an earthly way, almost as much as he loved the Lord. He thought back to Isaac's birth and how overjoyed they were to finally have their little earth angel, their joy! Abraham knew all children were angels from God, but he couldn't help but feel differently about his own son, the one who had come to them in their later years as a fulfilled promise from God.

He couldn't bear to think about Sarah and what she must be going through. Did he make a terrible mistake by not telling her exactly what the Lord was asking? Would doing the Lord's bidding be the end of her? He knew it would, for no mother is ever the same should they survive the untimely demise of their only child—especially one who has come to them so late in life and who was far too young to die.

Abraham had never felt so all alone in his over one hundred years of living! There he was, paralyzed, within inches of his beloved son, who was joy and gave him more of it than he had ever known before! He knew the act he was about to commit was against everything he had ever taught Isaac. Not only was it against the law of his nation, but because of the sneaky, underhanded way it was being carried out, it was against everything he stood for.

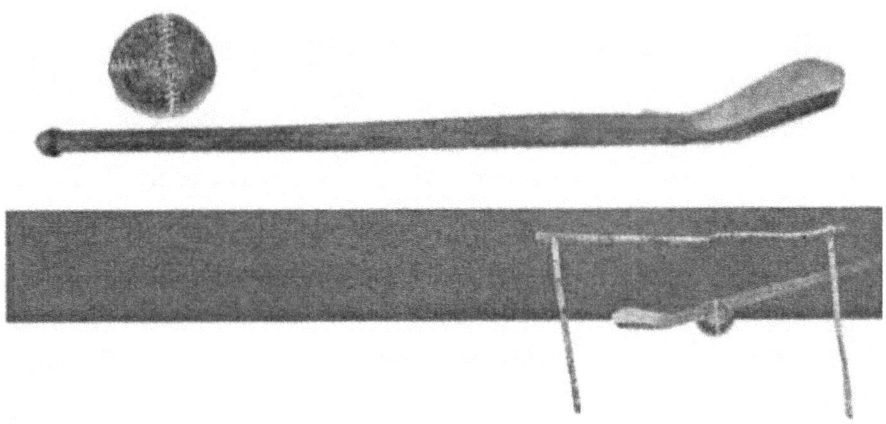

And there was Isaac, an arm's length away, wondering and worrying about the conclusion of this trip, yet trusting his father to take care of him as he always had. In desperation, Abraham prayed he would have the strength at that moment to overcome his paralysis and reach out and comfort his son. Just then, he felt his hand go out from him as he rested it on Isaac's shoulder. *Where did that come from,* he wondered? And then he knew he must trust and serve the Lord.

As for Isaac, his father's touch was all he needed. It soothed and comforted him like magic as if there was something greater in it.

Dawn came gradually over the mountains. By the time Isaac peeped his head out of the tent, he could see the three adults preparing something to eat and completing the tasks that would break camp and send them on their way.

"Wake up, sleepy head," Jabal shouted playfully at him.

In a moment, Isaac was over in the bushes making water like there was no tomorrow. He was so busy relieving himself that he didn't notice the snake slithering toward him from behind. It was an adder, whose bite was venomous and would surely mean death to one as young as he.

Fortunately for Isaac, Jabal was paying attention to more than his camp-breaking duties that morning. In an instant, the trusted servant hurled a rock at the snake, striking it just enough to alter its path away from Isaac, who couldn't stifle a yelp as he watched the serpent slither away.

The young lad thanked Jabal profusely for his attentiveness and quick action that may have saved his life. He immediately reported Jabal's good deed to his father, who thanked him also. But to the adults, the incident was more an opportunity for a desert learning experience than anything exciting, as it was to Isaac. He couldn't wait to get back to the settlement so he could tell his friends about his close call with a poisonous snake.

While walking back to his donkey, Isaac overheard Jubal say to his twin, "No one is safe as long as the evil snake crawls the earth!"

Jabal responded, "It has been so ever since the days of the garden, my brother."

Isaac soon learned the difference between traveling on the level desert floor and ascending a mountain. After a few hours of gradually more difficult riding, all four riders were on the ground leading their donkeys. Jabal and Jubal were now leading two animals each. The occasional glimpse of mountain goats helped bring home the obvious fact that the terrain they were climbing was not intended for human feet. They wondered at the gracefulness of the goats, who kept their distance while demonstrating their natural choreography on the slippery slopes. They saw

one of them slip, sending a few, smaller rocks tumbling below. It was a scary reminder of just how treacherous their trip was becoming.

The daydreaming of the day before was now replaced with constant apprehension. Their heightened state of awareness was a drain on them both mentally and physically. Isaac was grateful his father, though old in years, was still physically vigorous.

The higher they climbed the cooler the air became. They could see the summit of the mountain range was reachable in a day's climb. If luck stayed with them, they would be going down the other side before nightfall. The cooler air would enable them to keep going, whereas down below they would be forced by the heat to stop. All realized their thoughts must remain in the present. It's hard to worry about the future when your very next step could be your last! While Abraham preferred his present difficulties; they helped keep his mind off the trauma tomorrow would bring.

On they went, climbing higher and higher, through passages narrow and wide. At one point, the opening was so close the sides of the donkeys touched the rock as they went through. Abraham, Jabal, and their animals had already made it through one of these scary places when the group's silence was broken by the hungry growl of a mountain lion! The terrifying sound came from above and was so close to them that it caused Isaac to scream and jump in fear.

He wasn't the only one. The pack animals also rose up, braying loudly in response to imminent danger. None of them could believe how close and how loud the lion was; he was only a few feet above them! They couldn't grasp why one of them wasn't already in the clutches of the great beast.

Isaac looked over at the wide eyes of Jubal. Even this seasoned veteran of the mountains was clearly afraid, but his survival instincts took over. With Abraham and his twin already on the other side of the passage, he felt he had no choice but to motion for the young boy to precede him through the tiny entrance. With his spear at the ready, he signaled with his eyes and his arms for Isaac to lead his donkey toward him. At the same time, he brandished his spear upward at the hungry animal while issuing a throaty growl of his own. Jubal placed himself between Isaac and the terrifying beast while continuing to direct him toward the tiny opening. To his credit, young Isaac did not hesitate but immediately started to lead his donkey through the narrow gap.

Just then, they heard the roar of the mighty beast again. He had released himself from the rock and landed on his rear legs just behind Isaac's donkey, scraping the poor animal's rear flanks with his extended front claws as he fell. As his donkey went up on his hind legs, Isaac felt the reins he was holding tear through his fingers. Time stood still until Jubal grabbed him from the rear, carrying him through the narrow gap and quickly away from the ugly scene. The boy's last vision was the certain sacrifice his four-legged friend was about to make for him. The mammoth feline's claws were now digging into his donkey's sides; his huge, white

teeth were grasping at his bleeding neck. Neither time nor space would ever erase the screaming of his animal friend.

The group traveled quickly away from the lion's territory. Not even the rough terrain could shake the terrible scene from Isaac's mind. They all knew Isaac's faithful donkey had saved his life that day. He was filled with guilt and anxiety about his friend's sacrifice for him. He also realized that he owed his life to Jubal. The courageous twins had saved him twice in one day.

They were all grateful when Abraham decided to call for a short rest. His father came over to Isaac and placed his arm around him.

"Are you all right, my son? You have gone through a great deal this day."

Isaac wanted to break down and cry into his father's chest, but something inside him would not allow it.

Instead, he replied, "I will be okay, father. We are far away, but I cannot escape what I have seen and what happened to me back there."

"Do not try, brave one," Abraham responded. "The pictures you are seeing will dim, but the experience you have gained from this will make you stronger. Make your prayer of thanks to the Lord, and don't forget to include Jabal, Jubal, and your donkey in it. You have taken a giant step toward being a man today, my son."

Abraham made his remarks within the hearing of both his servants, men who were accustomed to both the dangers of battle and the desert. Their service and heroism for Abraham and his family were without question. Either one of them would have died for their ruler's son. Abraham's grateful glance at both of them was all that was needed to convey his deep appreciation. After a few more minutes of rest, Abraham gave the order to move on. Before many hours went by it would be dark. He wanted to be within the site of flatter land before then.

They reached the plateau of the mountain within an hour. The day's events made the feat almost anticlimactic. Nevertheless, they stopped for a few minutes to take in the view and savor the moment. The animals found little pockets of moisture on the surface of the summit, while the humans enjoyed a few drinks from their bladders of water. Isaac was still shaken, so Abraham gave him his first taste of wine in the hope that the potion would settle his nerves.

"After all, you will soon be a man," he said.

The strange liquid gave Isaac a warm feeling in his stomach and that was all. He could not stop thinking about the lion and his brave beast of burden. His mind could not find peace with the echoes of his donkey's screams so fresh in his memory.

The air on top of the mountain was chilly. All of them reached in their bags for additional clothing before taking off on their descent down the other side of the mountain. Abraham offered a quick prayer for a safe descent, and they were off.

"For a while, this may be even more difficult than coming up," their leader reminded them. "Have your ropes at the ready just in case."

There were only a few instances where they had to use their ropes to steady a descending climber. The going was very difficult, with the mules occasionally braying and baulking, but overall, the terrain seemed to be less steep than the other side of the mountain, with far fewer narrow passages to remind Isaac of his even narrower escape. Slowly, the land began to level off. They were still very much in the mountains but too exhausted to go farther. Thankfully, Abraham decided to use the remaining daylight to prepare for the evening's camp. They performed the evening chores as quickly as possible, said their prayers, and were soon asleep.

Isaac awoke to the now familiar sounds of the three older men breaking camp. As he shook the cobwebs from his brain, he suddenly remembered his near-death experience from the day before. He was surprised but happy that he recalled no nightmares from his sleep. Quite the contrary, he couldn't remember being so rested or feeling so peaceful, except that he could faintly remember these feelings when he was very young.

And then last night's dream came to him. No one spoke in his dream; words would have been a barrier to this heavenly communication. He was alone with God and his angels, but he couldn't describe them in any visual way. He saw and felt the glow and warmth of their presence. If there was a language being used, it was all in feelings, like the way he felt when his father comforted him last night. As wonderful as it felt to be close to God, he also had the distinct knowledge that he was still a long way from him, that someday he would come even closer to him. There was no message—only the wonderful feeling of peace and tranquility that lingered with him.

The third morning would be different for all the travelers. Jabal and Jubal, while attending their morning duties, were aware of the change in both Abraham and Isaac. They detected their calmness, and at the same time noticed their master seemed to be searching for something.

They rode along in this manner for several hours when suddenly Abraham turned to the trusted twins and said, "Stay here with the donkeys while I and the boy go over there. We will make our sacrifice now." Abraham loaded the wood for the burnt offering in a carrier and placed it over his son's back. He carried the box of hot coals and the knife.

The two of them went on together. Isaac spoke up, "Father?"

"Yes, my son?" Abraham replied.

"The fire and wood are here," Isaac said, "but where is the lamb for the burnt offering?"

Abraham answered, "God will provide the lamb for the burnt offering, my son." The two of them went on together.

When they reached the place God had told him about, Abraham built an altar there and arranged the wood on it. Hesitating, the father looked at his son. In that instant, their two resolves met, and Isaac knew he would be sacrificed for the Lord. Immediately, his mind raced back to yesterday's horrifying scene with the attacking lion. In a flash, he re-lived every agonizing moment of his brave friend's sacrifice for him. He could hear his screaming and feel the gashes from the attacker's claws; he could feel

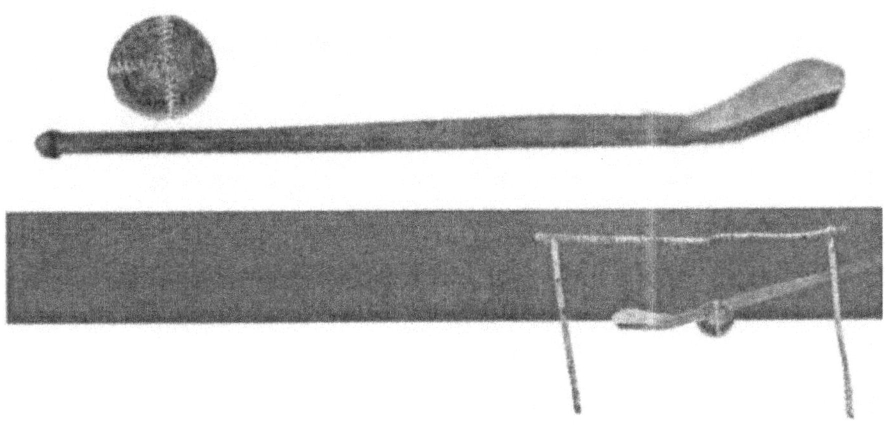

his own eyes widening in the same terror his donkey felt; his neck, where his father's knife would soon pierce, was already red hot and pulsating from within. Flashing in the sun, Isaac saw both Abraham's knife and the lion's sharp incisors' about to descend on him. Searching for his father's eyes, his mind was torn between earthly terrors and eerie acceptance of his sacrificial fate.

Abraham had positioned himself directly over the altar and his only son's helpless body. He summoned all his courage and energy to answer his God's command. Still averting his son's pleading eyes, with hands raised high above his head, he gathered himself to plunge the gleaming weapon.

But the angel of the Lord called out to him from heaven, "Abraham! Abraham!"

"Here I am," he replied.

"Do not lay a hand on the boy," he said. "Do not do anything to him. Now I know that you fear God because you have not withheld from me your son, your only son."

Abraham looked up, and, there in a thicket, he saw a ram caught by its horns. He went over and took the ram and sacrificed it as a burnt offering instead of his son. So Abraham called that place, The Lord Will Provide. And to this day, it is said, "On the mountain of the Lord it will be provided."

The angel of the Lord called to Abraham from heaven a second time and said, "I swear by myself, declares the Lord, that because you have done this and have not withheld your son, your only son, I will surely bless you and make your descendants as numerous as the stars in the sky and as the sand on the seashore. Your descendants will take possession of the cities of their enemies, and through your offspring, all nations on earth will be blessed because you have obeyed me."

Compared to all that had gone before, the journey home seemed uneventful. There were no more encounters with lions or snakes, and the few close calls they had in the mountains were taken almost in stride. In a strange way, the mountains felt more a part of Isaac. Now he knew how his father, Jabal, Jubal, and the rest of the adults from his tribe felt about their home in the desert and the mountains. He loved how his father had named the place where they encountered God, The Lord Will Provide, and how Jabal and Jubal, when they heard the story, said with one voice, "On the mountain of the Lord, it will be provided."

On the way back from there, Abraham and Isaac had said very little to each other. They didn't have to. After their encounter with God, no explanations were needed. Yahweh had tested Abraham's love and loyalty to him and found him steadfast as ever. Abraham and Sarah continued to be the right couple upon which to build a great nation. Isaac and the rest

of their nation's descendants would be blessed by the Lord because of Abraham's faith in God and Isaac's obedience to that faith.

As for Isaac, he knew he would never be the same. His life had been touched by God in a way that few humans ever would be. The calm that Yahweh had given him, both in his dream and during the time he lay on his father's altar, was still with him. He didn't know what would happen to him when he saw his father's knife flash in the sun, but he knew he had already given his life to the Lord. It was his to do with as he pleased. The only regret he felt was for his sweet mother. He wished he could have explained to her that everything was okay with him, that the Lord does indeed work in mysterious ways; and that he was at peace with his decision. In other words, he was, if it was God's will, ready to return to him in heaven.

Their return trip was made in slightly less time than their outward one. The twins found a safer route around the lion's pass. In the late morning of the third day, the exhausted riders could make out the dim silhouette of Sarah. It was as if she had never moved from their previous image of her. She was framed against the background of their settlement. The outlines of their tents were just barely visible behind her. Neither Abraham nor Isaac would speculate too soon, but in their hearts, they knew it was her. Both of them had thought of little else but her for the past few hours.

Sarah had started her vigil for the return of her husband, her son, and the twin servants early that morning. While gazing off into the dim horizon, she had spent the time fasting and praying. When she could barely make out the distant travelers, she started walking toward them. She moved slowly at first, her pace then quickening to match theirs. The last few yards were continued in a crescendo of happiness that found them all hugging and kissing each other. The two servants observed the scene with equal joy. Their gleeful smiles spread across their faces. Even the donkeys celebrated the reunion by nervously stomping in the sand.

First, Abraham explained to her what had taken place on the far side of the mountains, ending with, "So you see my love, by loving and trusting the Lord, we have secured his blessings for our people for generations to come."

Sarah gasped when she heard the news that Isaac was almost sacrificed by Abraham. She reached out and hugged her son even closer to her, staring into his eyes as if she couldn't believe he was finally home with her.

Then, excitedly, she explained, "I was so worried that I was sick! I couldn't eat or sleep thinking about all the dangers waiting for all of you in the mountains, let alone what would befall Isaac when you reached your destination. My mother's instinct told me the trip had something to do with our son. Come. Let's walk as we talk. You are all tired and need to bathe. After you rest, the entire tribe will prepare a feast and a celebration the likes of which have never been seen before, for the Lord has blessed us again! It was a wondrous miracle of the Lord!" Sarah exclaimed. "Please tell me more about it!"

During the mile or so left before they reached the settlement, Abraham and Isaac briefed their mother on just about everything that had occurred. (Upon Abraham's urging, the men had previously agreed to leave out many of the gory details of the lion's attack.) After Isaac explained the calm Yahweh had given him in his dream, Sarah interrupted him.

"Yes, my son. I am also familiar with the Lord's calming intervention. It was about this same time that I too was given his peace in a dream. Before that time, I was so upset with worry that I seriously considered going after you in the mountains by myself!"

Isaac responded, "Mother, not being able to speak with you was torture for us. With father, I prayed your mind would be soothed."

"Your prayers were answered, my sweet blessing," she responded. "And now our joy is complete, and you are nearly a man. Let us give thanks to the Lord."

Then Isaac recognized the familiar forms of many of his friends running toward them. Since the two servants had gone before them to meet their families, some of the boys had already heard a brief telling of their incredible story. They were falling all over each other with nervous excitement. Somehow, little Seth found himself leading the pack, his wide grin still in place exactly as Isaac remembered it.

Isaac was overcome with happiness as he ran to meet them. They met in a perfect scrum of joy, each boy fighting to grasp a piece of Isaac, who was now as much their spiritual leader as he was the head of their gang. As usual, they all ended up on the ground, laughing and screaming with the kind of bliss only the young can possess.

Enosh shouted above the fray, "Long live Isaac, for he has seen the Lord!"

Abraham and Sarah fought back tears of pride and joy as they viewed what would someday be the future of their nation. Then they quietly rode on to face the adult version of what had just taken place with Isaac's friends. By the time they reached the settlement, a large crowd had gathered at the base of a steep rise.

The joyful throng parted for them as they rode their donkey to the top of the rise. Abraham dismounted and then helped Sarah to the ground. By this time, the story had spread like a sandstorm through the desert. Abraham and Sarah stood there smiling and waving. They were never so happy to be at the head of such a great nation. Several elders of the tribe came forward to take their places beside them. After a while, the elders began to motion for quiet. By this time, the crowd had grown to several thousand.

Abraham, although exhausted by his six-day ordeal, was refreshed by the excitement of the throng. As he motioned for them to be still, he felt at one with them and was renewed by their energy. He looked toward Sarah as he raised his hands one more time for quiet. The people of the desert and the mountains became silent. Abraham's voice came to them as clear as the call of the desert hawk.

"Let us give thanks to the Lord."

The crowd responded, "We give thanks to the Lord."

Abraham continued. "We are here to give testimony to what came to be on the mountain of the Lord. My family and our trusted servants represented all of you in what has come to pass as Yahweh's test of our mutual faith. Many times I wanted to turn away from the horrible task the Lord had set me on. I prayed to him for strength as I borrowed it from my family and each and every one of you. Because you were in our hearts and because we are as one nation, Yahweh will continue to bless us in the time to come, for he has said, 'I will surely bless you and make your descendants as numerous as the stars in the sky and as the sand on the seashore. Your descendants will take possession of the cities of their enemies and through your offspring, all nations on earth will be blessed, because you have obeyed me.'"

With this, the crowd erupted in cheers. When they quieted down, Abraham finished with these words: "Remember, when your faith is sorely tested, that your needs will be provided on the mountain of the Lord. Let us give thanks and praise to the Lord."

The young Hebrew nation came back in unison, "Let us give thanks and praise to the Lord."

And so what started out to be the fulfillment of a great tragedy turned into one of the happiest times in the history of Abraham and Sarah's people. The Lord had indeed provided as he did for the following feast and celebration, which took many hours to prepare and went on for an entire week! No people had ever been so close to their God nor celebrated that special bond so joyously. There was feasting, games, plays, storytelling, special prayers of thanks, and athletic events such as running and jumping, and stone-throwing. And when they were finished with all of that, they simply started the cycle of celebration all over again until they were exhausted with it after a week's time.

# THE BIG GAME

But not all hearts were touched in equal thanksgiving and happiness. Isaac's thrust into tribal prominence as one of the main stars in the story their nation was celebrating had set Tubal off on a tirade of anger and bitterness. Isaac's newfound fame as the young man who was willing to give his life for his people was a tremendous blow to his ego.

While reeling from Isaac's new popularity, he happened to overhear Magog, one of his own gang, agreeing with the praise that was being heaped on Isaac. Upon hearing this, he proceeded to beat the unfortunate lad so severely with his staff that he was laid up for several days, telling his parents that he had fallen from a cliff. But the rest of Tubal's followers knew the truth and wondered which one of them would be next.

During the time of celebration, Tubal did everything he could to keep his small band close to him. He was so quick to give a cuff to the back of the head that his partners in intimidation began standing more than an arm's length away from him. They were all "cuff shy" and growing weary of his vile temper. If the truth were to be known, the supreme bully had already lost the hearts of his followers. Now he was fighting to keep the rest of their bodies on his side.

To make matters even worse, the Raiders, in many of the celebratory games and events, were not faring nearly as well as they used to when competing against Isaac's Hornets. It was clear that whatever happened to Isaac while he was gone had given him some kind of strange powers. These new powers were enhancing his athleticism even more and surrounding him with an aura of invincibility that was apparent to all. Tubal thought Isaac even looked taller and stronger. Isaac's new enthusiasm was spreading among the Hornets. Tubal knew he would have to act fast if his side was going to prevail in the upcoming "Challenge" match, which they scheduled for the day after tomorrow. To his way of thinking, drastic times called for drastic measures.

That night, things seemed to play into his hands. They were out looking for ways to cause trouble when they spotted Isaac on his way home. They saw him duck into a little-known trail that could be used as a shortcut to his quarters. Tubal quickly gave orders for several boys to run ahead and block Isaac's way, while he and the remainder of his gang started to follow from behind. The two groups converged on Isaac in a narrow passageway surrounded by rocks. The scene reminded Isaac of the lion's attack, but this time there would be no rescue by Jabul and no escaping a confrontation with his enemies.

There was no time for the trapped boy to think or even react. While he was measuring the group in front of him, the cowardly Tubal struck the back of Isaac's head with his staff. He saw his tormentor's face as he collapsed backward, blood streaming down his neck. Tubal let out a yell and ordered all to attack the body writhing in pain and helpless on the ground. The blows rained down on the son of Abraham, rendering him unconscious, which did not stop Tubal from meeting out even more punishment. The descendant of Cain was about to verify the killing of his nemesis when the gruesome scene was interrupted by the sound of voices and footsteps coming from behind them. In a flash, Tubal and his henchmen were gone. They were confident Isaac would never rise again.

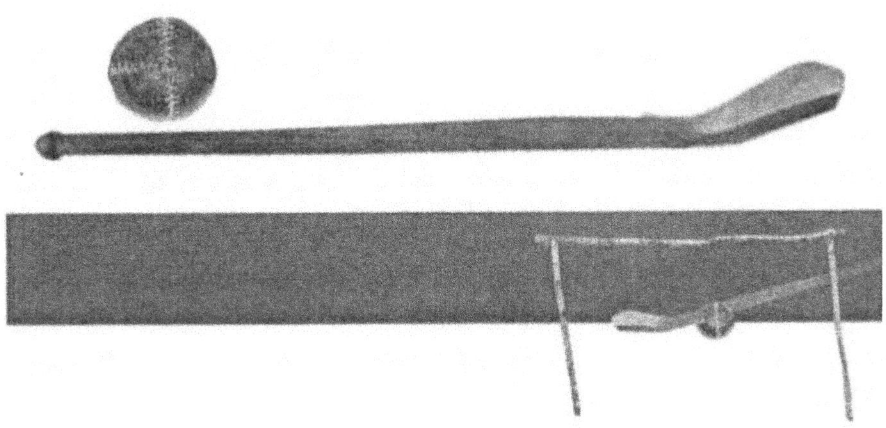

This time little Seth played an even greater role in the life of his idol. As the very young are want to do, he rarely took his eyes off his hero. Earlier, when Isaac split off from his friends to go home, the young boy made the decision to hang back from a turn so he could watch Isaac as long as possible. He could easily catch up with the others. By hanging back, he was the only one to see Isaac take the shortcut that might also shorten his life.

Something also made little Seth stay back yet another moment longer. As he did, he caught a glimpse of Tubal and his gang coining into view. When he saw the rival gang split off and their leader's group start toward the entrance to Isaac's shortcut, he immediately ran for his friends. They had gotten farther ahead than he thought and were just about to split up when he caught them. His frantic plea to help their leader was barely out of his mouth before all of them were off and running. Although little Seth was very young, they trusted his intuition above all others in the group.

The boy's hearts sank as Isaac's rumpled body came into view. When Enosh turned him over and everyone saw the blood covering his neck, little

Seth began to cry and scream his fallen hero's name. Lying there, motionless, it appeared to all that the one they all loved the most was dead. A chorus of whaling began. It was low at first and then slowly rose in volume and emotion. Slowly, repeatedly, they joined young Seth in calling Isaac's name. "Isaac! Isaac! Isaac ..." they moaned like sheep calling their own.

The chorus went on, each boy praying to God that it wasn't true when suddenly they saw Isaac stir in Enosh's arms. All became very still in order to hear their leader's painful whisper.

"What's all the whining about? Can't I get some sleep around here?"

The boys burst out in a cheer! Their prayers were answered. Although nearly beaten to death by Tubal's gang, Isaac was indeed alive.

He was alive but still in extreme danger. The humorous message he barely managed to murmur took everything he had to give, and he soon slumped back into unconsciousness. It didn't seem to matter to his friends.

They had heard enough to give them hope and hope was all they needed to activate the tremendous faith they had in their captain. Somehow, someway, he would return to them.

Enosh and some of the older boys quickly formulated a plan to carry Isaac to safety. They took turns carefully carrying him to a tent that was normally used for the nurturing of newborn goats and sheep—those that had lost their mothers. Since it was the older boy's job to tend to these animals, they knew it was unlikely any adults would discover Isaac there. As for Isaac, he was moaning again, but he had not regained consciousness.

It was getting late, so they sent one of the boys to the tent of Abraham and Sarah to ask permission for their son to spend the night with Enosh's family. They knew this permission was routinely given because the boys frequently spent nights with each other's families. It was so matter of fact that all they had to do was inform the guards, who would, depending on the hour, sometimes even wait until the morning to inform Sarah.

This process was repeated throughout the ranks of the older boys until a cadre of attendants was created. It would be the responsibility of these boys to take turns tending to Isaac for the remainder of the night. They would watch over him; see the compress for his head was fresh, his wounds were clean, and that he would have fresh water. They would also make sure the newborn kids and lambs did not disturb him, which seemed unlikely since several of them were already snuggled up to him as gentle as, well, a lamb.

Before the younger boys were sent off to their tents, Isaac's second-in-command gathered everyone together for a prayer of healing.

"Dear Lord, please hear our plea. We implore you to be with us tonight as we watch over Isaac. You remember him, the boy that was willing to give his life for all of us on the other side of your mountain. We trust in you, oh Lord, and know that if it is your will, then our best friend will come back to us. Amen, Lord."

Then little Seth piped up, "Yes, Lord, and please give Old Oneball a big, black eye tonight, will you?"

Their laughter caused Isaac to stir. It was either that or the newborn kids licking his wounds. One of them was aggressively working on the cut and swelling on the back of his head, while the others licked his sore ankle and the rest of his body. This process seemed natural to the boys, so they let it go on.

Just before the little ones left, Isaac opened his eyes for the second time. No words came out, but he did manage a weak smile. The gang took it as another sign.

The night also wore on for Tubal. Lying in his tent, he knew he would be in big trouble if the adults found out he was responsible for the attack on their "Little Hero." Just thinking about Isaac made him want to go back and "finish the job," if it wasn't finished already. Too bad he didn't have a little more time back there in the passageway. He would have made sure little mommy's boy never got up again.

He couldn't sleep, so he thought he would go out and check on Tiras. He had posted him just outside his tent in case he needed a warning to make a quick getaway from the adults or one of Isaac's avenging friends. He felt like he needed to hit somebody and Tiras would be an easy target. He knew he would catch him either nodding off or about ready to.

He snuck up behind him. His shout startled him so much that Tiras automatically swung around with his staff and hit the tyrant very hard right over his right eye! The pain was so intense the woozy giant could not recover enough to administer a revenge hit on his lieutenant. All he could do was manage to stumble back into his tent before passing out on his

bedding For better or for worse, Tubal was down for the count and out for the night. Tiras would have to stew about his punishment until morning, but for the moment, he felt better about the pain his leader was suffering.

Isaac was startled awake by the pungent odor of lamb farts in his nostrils. He didn't know how long they had been building there, but he did remember feeling the little bleaters rear ends cuddled right up to his nose. Was this the cause of his splitting headache, lamb stinkers?

He closed his eyes again and felt the pain in the back of his head. Then it all started to come back to him. He remembered his shortcut, the dark passage way, running into some of Tubal's gang in front of him, and the blow from behind. He remembered the heinous expression on Tubal's face as he went down and then his friends saying something to him. He started to figure out what happened to him and why he would be where he was—lying on straw next to cuddly little lambs and goats with bad breath coming out both ends.

When the boy on watch saw Isaac moving around, he called for Enosh and the rest of their gang. Within a few minutes, they were all on hand celebrating the news that Isaac was at least conscious again. They helped Isaac sit up and watched eagerly as he downed some water. No eyes were ever more eager for positive signs than the ones watching their role model.

His friend's quick queries—"How do you feel, Isaac?" "Where does it hurt?"—gave the brave lad all he could handle for the moment.

"It would be easier to tell you where I don't hurt," was Isaac's much slower reply. "Give me a couple of hours to clear some of this fog from my head, and then we will have a strategy session. In the meantime, I suggest you head over to the practice field and give yourselves a short workout. Be sure to post a lookout. We will try to postpone today's match with the devil and his forces, but there is no guarantee we can get that done."

Then Enosh explained all that had taken place before and after the attack, giving special emphasis to little Seth's role in saving their hero's life. He explained that Tubal, knowing he had them on the run with Isaac out of the picture, would not allow them to reschedule the match. "He told us he would kill every one of our pets if we didn't show up for the game today!" exclaimed Enosh.

Isaac was moved by what little Seth had done for him. He called to him and put his arm around him, saying, "From this day forward, we shall no longer call you Tittle,' but by your rightful name only." He hugged him right there in front of everyone, which gave Seth a warm feeling of pride and joy that all of them shared.

Then Isaac called for Lightning. With great pain and effort, he pulled himself up from the ground. Leaning on his trusty staff, he said, "Friends, after what has happened to me, it is clear with Tubal we are not dealing with someone who fears Yahweh. It is also clear that the mark of Cain is upon him and that he thirsts for the blood of his next victim. We must act accordingly. We have no time for lengthy plans. Thanks to all of you and

our wooly friends, I am alive and with you. But I am in no condition to play a game of "Challenge," especially one with so much at stake. When I fail to show at the field today, Tubal will think I am dead. This will work to our advantage when the time comes. You will spread the word that you haven't seen me since last night. Should the Raider's win today, Tubal's future reign of terror will no doubt include the taking of human life. Let us pray."

With that, the boys knelt to the ground. Isaac continued, "Our plan must be God's plan. He has said, 'The Lord will provide.' We have faith that our victory will be provided also, and we must play in the glory of his name. Amen."

"Amen," the boys replied.

Their leader, his strength slowly ebbing away, went on. "Now, get some food and plenty of water inside you. Try to relax and stay calm. We must play for the joy of playing and not for the despair of revenge. You will see me when and if it is Yahweh's will."

The boys disbanded, their heads held a little higher than before Isaac's words. Isaac leaned on Ole Lightning for as long as he could, while watching his friends disappear down the hill. Seth crooked his head back so far to keep gazing at Isaac that he tripped over his own feet and tumbled the rest of the way down the hill. The boy's screams of laughter greeted him when he finally came to rest. One of them teased him, "Come along, Seth. There's nothing little about your feet either."

Tubal woke up that morning with a throbbing pain in his right eye and a fervent desire for revenge, which immediately caused him to spring into action. When he tore open the flap of his tent, he expected to seeTiras, the object of his murderous desires. Instead, he saw Japheth, a much smaller boy who knew the story and looked as if he was about to be eaten for breakfast.

"Please don't hit me, Tubal. I'm only here filling in for Tiras," the boy pleaded.

"Where is that piece of dog dung?" he demanded. "I'm looking to push him off a cliff before this day is over."

The boy replied, "The last time I saw him he was headed that way." He pointed toward the mountains.

"Good. That will make it easier for me." I Ic finished the conversation by ordering the boy to soak a rag in cool water and bring it to him. He waited for him to turn his head in the opposite direction before he cuffed him from behind. The blow sent the lad sprawling and gave Tubal short relief from his throbbing eye pain. Now he was in a better mood.

His new mood lasted about as long as it took him to feel the sting of his eye again, but he couldn't afford the luxury of nursing his pain. He had things to do, like annihilate what was left of Isaac's gang during the afternoon "Challenge" match. He was comforted by the knowledge that the game was just a pretense for his team to beat up on their smaller opponents. With Isaac out of the way, playing them would be as easy as

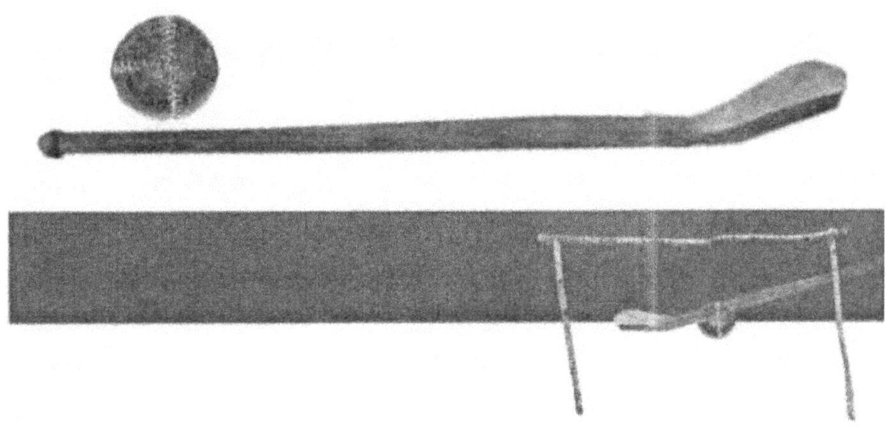

finding sand in the desert. He couldn't wait to be the undisputed ruler of his little kingdom again.

As for Isaac, Tubal's sources told him he was nowhere to be found. After questioning some of Isaac's friends, several of his people reported back that none of them had seen him. And because of all the festival-related sleepovers among the young people, Isaac's parents and the rest of the adults were unlikely to miss him for a long while. Suddenly, the fiend broke out into a maniacal laugh. He had just conjured up the image of Sarah's pretty boy being torn to bits by desert jackals. By the time they were done with his body, there would be nothing left but bones. Life was good again for Tubal.

Isaac had used every ounce of his energy in giving his talk. It was all he could do to get back into his shelter and lie down, where he fell asleep for several hours. When he awoke, he felt much better until he tried to get up again. Then he realized there would be no miraculous recoveries. A potion one of the boys had given him earlier seemed to dull the pain, until he tried to walk. When he put too much weight on his left side, the pain was just too much to continue the effort without support from his staff.

After drinking some fresh water, he sat back down to think about his dilemma - to play or not to play. On the one hand, he knew if he didn't play, the contest would be a massacre. His boys would play bravely, but Tubal would make sure the game was so physical there could only be one outcome: the Raiders win the physical contest easily. On the other hand, if he showed up in full view with his team, they would gain from the surprise of his presence but would soon lose that gain once he started trying to put too much weight on his left side—advantage lost. No matter how hard he tried, he couldn't come up with a plan. He sat there stewing about it for a long time before he gave his worries to Yahweh:

*Dear Lord, I know you see what's happening. The forces of evil are poised to score a great victory over us unless you intervene in some way. I stillfeel your presence within and know you will be with us. We will trust and serve the Lord.*

Young Isaac still did not have a plan, but he believed in his prayer, and he believed in the Lord. With the time of the match approaching, he asked one of the boys to send for the rest of their friends. There in front of them, leaning on Lightning, he said, "Remember, we play for the joy of the game and for all that is good in us. I will be watching, but I will not be on the field with you."

Hearing this, the group gave a collective groan.

He continued. "The wounds inflicted on me by the cowardly Tubal have not healed enough to allow me to compete with you today. I ask you to think about how I was wounded—from behind. He was afraid to face

me just as he will fear your courage today. We will win this match as much from the effort of those off the field as those on the field. So that our players on the field are forewarned, those of you on the sidelines will be the eyes in the back of their heads. When you sec an attack coming from the rear, you will, all of you at once, shout the name of the person about to be attacked. This will give them the split second they need to respond. Be vigilant. Without you, they are doomed.

"Enosh will lead you on the field as he has lead you most of the way. Feel his courage and determination. I will be watching from behind the rocks and the tamarisk to the right of the field until such time as the Lord will provide. Let us pray together." Isaac bowed his head, praying, "Lord, watch over us today as we compete in your name. We know the Raiders will break all of the rules. Give us extra strength and courage to stop them so that we can bring you victory. Amen."

"Amen," they all responded.

It was time. Enosh called for his team to file into ranks of threes and begin marching the distance between them and the field. They would enter the field of play in an orderly manner, with pride and dignity. Isaac would follow as best he could and then disappear into the rocks when the time came. Soon after they started, Seth began whistling a familiar tune. The march and the tune calmed them and made them feel as one. When they entered the playing area, they saw their opponents at the opposite end of the field. Tubal, the towering giant, stood defiantly in front of his Raiders.

As they drew closer, the lead Hornets began to notice there was something different about Tubal's right eye. Kenan was the first one to see it for what it was: a shiner so large and so bright the sun reflected off its surface. With his good eye swollen shut, Tubal's angled left eye reflected a deep evil, frightening to behold yet almost impossible to turn away from.

Enosh exclaimed, "Good heavens! Seth, you've got your wish! He's has a black eye the size of a fist! They all began to laugh as they marched, stopping right in front of the opposing team.

Tubal was immediately outraged by their mocking laughter. His response was to continue what he was doing to entertain himself and his team while they waited. That afternoon his side had managed to steal Seth's pet lamb. His plan, if the other side didn't show for the match, was to fulfill his threat and make the poor animal his first victim. Out of sheer cruelty, he ordered his players to make a loop on the end of a straw rope and tie it around the animal's head. From a box lined with rock, they produced a hot coal. Amidst Seth's and his teammate's screams, Tubal lit the end of the straw rope. He laughed with glee as the little lamb bleated in fear and began running toward the rocks, his fiery demise gaining on him as he went. It was more than Seth could take! He quickly broke ranks with his friends and chased after his beloved pet, calling him as he went.

After the name-calling had died down, both forces were more than motivated for the match to end all matches. Someone threw a ball onto the center of the field and the game was on. Those not starting the match quickly lined opposing sides of the field.

Tubal and a few of his bigger players led the charge for their team. With wide eyes and nostrils flaring, they used their staffs more for pushing and shoving than passing the ball. It was clear the giant had given his team orders to play rough or risk his wrath. They were all under his evil spell—especially when he was on the "Challenge" field urging them to commit every foul they could.

Enosh and his boys played gallantly, but they could not match the size of their opponents, nor their ferocity. They could tell the Raiders were buoyed by Isaac's absence, with Tubal constantly shouting, "Where's your pretty boy now?"

Within minutes, the tyrant had easily scored the first goal. Without Isaac to stand up to his dirty tricks, all he had io do was wait until his team members got the ball somewhere near their goal. From that point, he simply held the ball against the ground with his club head and walked it over to the goal, where he physically picked the goalie up with his other arm and swept the ball into the goal. There was nothing the Hornets could do about it.

Enosh would not allow his team to succumb to the tactics of a dictator. He had made up his mind. The next time he committed an infraction, he was going to confront him. He knew he risked leaving his team without a leader on the field. Should Tubal decide to "Take him out" physically, his team would be abandoned. He would have to take the risk.

After the evil one's haughty goal, Enosh called for a time out. He gathered his entire team around him while their opponents taunted them with epitaphs. "Chicken dung," "Goat turds," and "Mommy's boys," were a few of the calls they tried to ignore while Enosh spoke to them.

"The next time the cheater pulls something like that, I'm going to stand up to him. If he takes me out, you must remain calm and keep your minds in the game. Ur, if that happens, you will take charge of the team. The Raiders are so cocky right now it is hard to deal with them. All we can do is stay focused and try to put some pressure on them. From now on, we will go to our 'platoon' play. Remember, fresh legs feed the wolf. We will wear them out with our passing and our defense. Our only chance is to stay in this game long enough to make a difference in the end. Remember our prayer."

With that, the boys broke up to the shout of "Hornets!" From now on, they would play as two teams, switching back and forth seamlessly on silent signal from their leader. The fresh team would blend into the field at the exact same time the other one was leaving it. If they pulled it off just right, their opponents would barely notice what was going on.

But nothing seemed to faze the giant one. He was at the top of his game—so drunk with power he was chuckling to himself on the sidelines before play resumed. For a moment, he even forgot about his black eye—that is until play started and Enosh bumped it with his elbow.

The pain caused a roar deep from his chest. His wound was now open, and blood was trickling down his right cheek. Mad with pain, he looked

around for someone to hurt. Because Enosh had gone on to the next play, he grabbed two of his own players and tried to slam their heads together. Thankfully for them, they sustained only a glancing blow before falling to the ground. Enosh's hit soon closed the Cyclops's injured eye, and he was starting to have problems with the vision in his remaining one.

While Tubal was reeling from all this, Enosh gave the signal for his rested squad to come in. The transition went smoothly. The new boys came in refreshed and ready to play. They were soon running, feinting, and passing like true hornets inside the hive—somehow communicating on a higher, inaudible level to keep from running into one another, while weaving their way down the field. It was all too dizzying and disorienting for the Raiders, who were starting to tire. In the next instant, they scored on a sharp pass to Kenan, and his even sharper slice shot on goal. It was now one to one. They erupted in cheers that turned Tubal's anger into resolve.

As bad as he hurt, he was in more than good enough shape to quell this little comeback. With club in hand, he marched right over to the Hornet's celebration. Approaching from behind as usual, he was about to strike Enosh on the back of the head in the same fashion he did Isaac. Partly because of his blurred vision and partly because of a last second warning yell from the direction of the rocks, his club hit the unsuspecting captain more on the neck and shoulder than the head. Still, he went down from the sheer force of it.

The mad Nephilim then straddled Enosh like a lion straddles his kill. He was daring all comers to take "it" away from him. With blood now smeared with sweat and cached to his face and hair, any human resemblance faded into wounded animal. None of the Hornets could bare to look into the pure evil emitting from Tubal's eye of death. He stood there triumphantly, even haughtily. He left no doubt his next move would be to drive his club as far into their friend's skull as he could. The standoff continued for what seemed an eternity.

Then several things happened at the same time. The Hornets, in unison and without verbal communication, started slowly stepping toward their fallen teammate. In response, Tubal began to raise his club up from behind his back. Just then, Seth, who had been hiding with Isaac, obeyed his order to dash to Enosh's rescue. He sprinted from the rocks and grabbed Tubal's wrists and arms before they could swing the monster's club down on Enosh's skull.

Seth's small frame was all the force needed to redirect Tubal's arms. He held on to them with all his might as he went sailing into the air. Seth landed in a ball at the feet of his friends. He quickly sprang up to join them in their slow advance toward Tubal.

Now the lion was clearly outnumbered by the jackals. Tubal gave a low, throaty sound and started to slowly back off from his prey. When the villain looked around for help from his gang, he found them at a distance, opened-eyed and agape after witnessing his retreat. They were stunned as

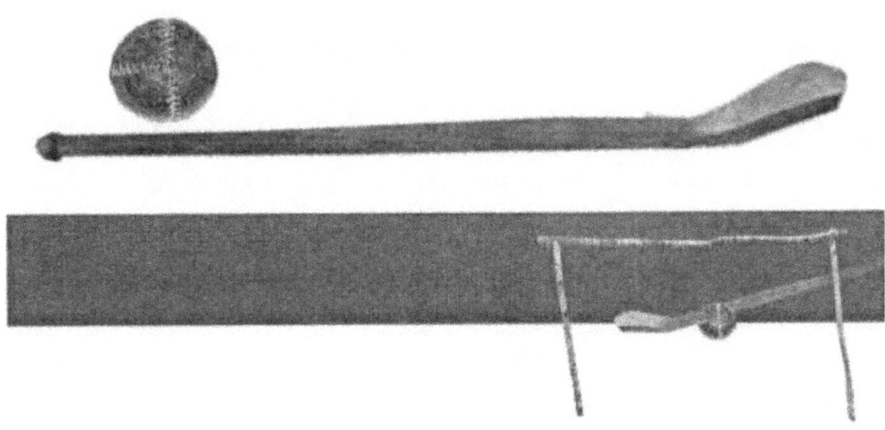

they watched their evil master fall back. Tubal yelled at them to join ranks, but they were too stunned from their master's retreat to respond.

Just then, Enosh threw the finest gallop ball any of them had ever seen toward the center of the field. Wounded, but already up from the ground, he cried, "Play ball!" The game was on again. Enosh was a sportsman; it was his desire to see their conflict settled on the field of play.

Even Tubal, who was embarrassed by his retreat in front of both teams, couldn't resist the call to re-join the game. He played with a vengeance that fed his anger but did nothing to reassure the rest of the Raiders. For the first time ever, they had seen him faced down by his enemies. That realization was too fresh in their minds. They could not recover from their leader's cowardly image and the fact he was now so mad they were as unsafe around him as the Hornets were. All of this combined to cause them to play with apprehension.

Suddenly, the smaller team, lifted by the gallantry of Enosh and the fresh legs and spirit of Seth, began to play with more energy than ever. With organization and clarity, they were everywhere on the field. They were passing, blocking, and shooting with rhythm and purpose. When one group tired, the other one would take over. Their last-second warning strategy had saved several of them. They were giving Isaac a show that made him beam with pride.

Even the giant one became less of a problem for the smaller but more eager team. Tubal was so weary from his wounds and trying to keep up with the game that his reaction time slowed. His breathing became even heavier. At the same time the Raiders were faltering the Hornets began to behave like their namesakes. They were buzzing their opponents from all directions in a dizzying performance of physical conditioning, talent, and skill.

On one occasion, Seth waited until his teammates dist racted Tubal long enough for him to hit him with his body on the back of his legs, causing the angry cyclops to crumple to the ground. The young boy's familiar grin after accomplishing this feat was priceless. His play gave them a burst of energy. After that, it was all the exhausted giant could do to crawl a few feet to the sidelines and try to catch his breath. He lay there with his eye bleeding, face up, chest heaving, lungs wheezing, and his mind reeling from the prospects of a possible defeat!

With Tubal down on the ground, it was easy for the Hornets to work their magic on the stunned Raiders. They took turns scoring goals until the score was six to four in favor of Enosh's squad.

From his vantage point, Isaac knew the game was far from over. He watched Tubal's body rising from the ground, where he had slowly regained strength and determination. He thought, *Beware the wounded giant.* At the same time, he was testing his weight against his left ankle,

where Seth's little friend had been licking him during the game. He was uncertain and nervous as he continued to pray, *The Lord will provide. The Lord will provide…*

Lying next to the field, Tubal was able to catch his breath and rest his limbs, while his mind took in the brilliant play of the Hornets. The more he saw, the angrier he became and the more determined he was to do something about it. To the bellow of, "Challenge! Challenge!" Tubal's hulking body rose from the ground. He was coming toward them, looking more inhuman than ever and demanding control of the ball. His maniacal, one-eyed look frightened them anew. Someone was going to pay the price for the Hornets' comeback.

That someone turned out to be Seth—pound for pound perhaps the most courageous of all the hornets. When he saw the blood-spattered giant approaching his team, he immediately stepped forward and stood knee to nose with him, looking up defiantly at the face of evil. If the scene hadn't been so dangerous, it would have been comical. The rest of the Hornets were in awe of their young friend's bravery and began to shout their encouragement before they all stepped forward to join him.

This time, Tubal would have none of the team jackal defense. When Seth turned around in grinning acknowledgement to his teammates, the brute gave him a running kick to his midsection, sending him flying many cubits into the air. He landed against the rocks, his head snapping against them with a sickening thud. He lay there, barely conscious.

Tubal gave the stunned Hornets no time to show sympathy for their fallen friend. A moment later, he waded into them. His left arm was flailing at them while he clumsily maneuvered the ball with his club. He took his time among them, enjoying every cuff and kick he got in, even smiling a few times when the blows he landed were especially hard ones. He was jubilant when he took Enosh out of the competition with a vicious strike to his midsection.

After Isaac's lieutenant went down, the sting went completely out of the Hornets. He finished the rest of them off with ease. Ail that was left was the formality of Tubal breaking the plane of the abandoned goal with the ball. He accomplished the task with a flare and then turned to witness the havoc he had wrought among the Hornets, most of whom were scattered on the ground. Tubal's team was also scattered, afraid to be near him even in victory. The victorious cheater let out a mighty roar of triumph, which seemed to shake the Earth as it settled deep into the hearts of all the boys.

It seemed to be a very good day for the tyrant. 1 I is only rival was dead. He was now undisputed king of the desert, master of all the youth of the tribe. All of them would be at his beck and call, forced to wait on him hand and foot. The thought of that prospect gave him hunger pangs. He remembered he hadn't drank or eaten for some time. As he sauntered toward the other end of the field, he looked around for someone to take his food and drink order. Enosh and Seth, recovering from their wounds at the same time, would make ideal waiters for him.

All became very quiet, each one in deep despair, contemplating how poor their futures would be under their ever-growing tumor of a tyrant. Time came to a terrifying stop. Everyone waited in silence for their renewed ruler's first command.

But the sound of a lamb's bleating broke the silence as sharply as an eagle's cry. The Hornets recognized it as the sound of hope, while Tubal heard it with contempt. The hungry giant immediately knew what was going to still his hunger pangs.

They all looked in the direction of the rocks, where they saw Isaac appear. While trying not to limp, he was holding Lightning in one hand and Seth's pet in the other, his bleating growing louder the closer they came. Time and place could not contain the magnitude of emotions that swelled up in everyone. All were in shock. The Hornets, who had been lost in their own valiant effort and resounding defeat, somehow managed to come to attention. As wounded as their leader was earlier in the day, they thought he could have passed out again from his pain or succumbed to his head injury.

Isaac had continued watching, while praying he would have the courage to overcome his pain and venture into the teeth of the tyrant, who had just defeated his brave friends. It seemed the more Seths pet licked his ankle the better it felt, so he let the process go on as long as he could. It got to the point where he at least trusted his weight on it. He could walk, but he knew he could not run. His plan would have to work.

Tubal thought he was seeing a ghost! He stood there statue like, his mouth so far open a bird could perch on it. Before the bully could change his emotions from the pride he had in his victory to the shock he felt in seeing a dead person, Isaac decided to take the initiative.

"Hello, Oneball," Isaac spoke in mock cheerfulness. Just then, the little lamb leaped from his arm to join his master. Isaac held Lightning up in the air and shouted "Challenge!" as loud as he could. The shout gave a spark of courage and energy to the Hornets. When Enosh saw what was happening, he immediately rolled Isaac's new ball so that it stopped right in front of their captain.

Tubal, recovering from the sight of Isaac standing valiantly in front of him was in the perfect position in terms of distance and angle to think any shot on goal would have to go right through the middle of his immense body. He regained his wits enough to let out a sinister laugh and yell, "Mommy's boy is back! And now I get the pleasure of beating him all over again."

The mammoths first step toward Isaac was in sync with Isaacs backswing. In preparation for the shot, he had already aligned himself to Tubal's left, which made him think he might pass the ball off to one of the other Hornets. After Isaac swung down and rotated his forearms through to his finish position, the ball did indeed sail out toward his friends near their side of the field. Then everyone watched in amazement as the ball turned suddenly and sharply left. It wasn't until then that Tubal realized the possibility of the ball going anywhere near the untended goal. But the

very next instant brought it home to him—not only was it going near the goal; it was on path to go in it!

All watched for what seemed the longest time. They were in awe of the shot and what was to happen next. When the ball finally broke the plane of the goal, the Hornets erupted in a cheer of victory that made their earlier celebrations look mild. The entire team was on Isaac in a few seconds. They were screaming, jumping up and down, laughing, and hugging their hero. In one dazzling shot, he had taken them from the depths of despair to the heights of victory.

The hulk looked upon the scene with chilling humor. By now, he had figured out that Isaac was still crippled from his previous wounds and would be no match for him. Just because Isaac had pulled off some trick shot meant nothing to him. As long as he was standing this day, all future days would belong to him. With vengeance in mind, he prepared his staff and his body to wade in. He would seek Isaac and take him out first. The rest of the worn out Hornets would be easy.

But there were some things going on in all the boys minds which the dictator failed to recognize. In his lust for power, he failed to notice that his abusive tactics had pushed some of his own team too far. He thought he could always easily control them. He didn't know that Tiras, while hiding in the foothills, had come across Isaac and Seth. When he explained to them that he had accidentally struck his master in the eye with his staff and that the bully planned to push him off a cliff in revenge, their hearts went out to him. Isaac asked him to leave Tubal's gang and try to convince his friends to come with him. He told him that all of them could form new teams and play with and against different players from time to time. It was the right invitation at the right time.

In the aftermath of Tubals apparent victory, several of his team had wandered off into the hills. There they came upon Tiras. They told him they were afraid to be around their leader in victory, let alone defeat. Tiras explained to them what Isaac had said and repeated his offer to them. Like him, they were more than happy to accept Isaac's friendship. They were watching from a short distance also. Tiras told his friends they must be willing to risk everything in order to save Isaac. So when they saw their former leader preparing another attack on Isaac and his friends, they were prepared to counterattack.

Tiras had a stone in his slingshot ready for launching. The missile struck the giant in his right shoulder, just as he was about to raise his staff against Isaac. When he went down from the blow, his entire team turned on him. Those on the field didn't have to think very long before they joined their teammates, who were pouring out of the rocks to rescue Isaac.

The slingshot from Tiras would only stop Tubal for a moment, causing him to writhe on the ground in pain. His team had to act fast in order to subdue him for good. They did so by swarming him with their bodies, each one taking a small portion of the giant's own body and holding it down with all of their might. Even with their best effort, Isaac was forced to give the order for his own team to help hold the monster down. The order was hardly necessary. Remembering all his cuffs over the years, they couldn't

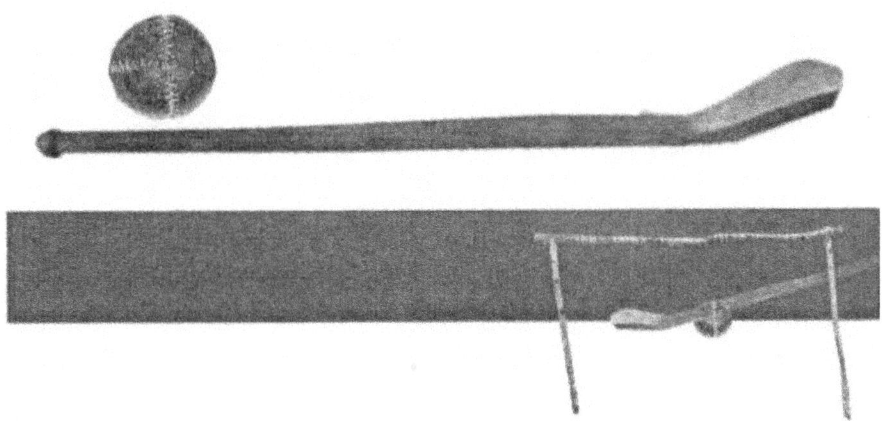

wait to pounce on the mad giant. They also couldn't resist a few kicks and punches to his ugly frame. Soon, the great villain was too exhausted to resist. He lay there, glued to the ground by the collective will of all those who used to fear him. His evil had finally worn out its welcome among those who were forced to suffer it.

Isaac ordered several of the younger boys to get some heavy stakes and rope. They drove the stakes in the ground around the hulk's perimeter and tied his huge limbs to them. Until the adults were informed of his evil ways, he wasn't going anywhere. The tribal council would have to deal with him tomorrow, because the boys decided, for better or for worse, Tubal would spend the night staked out on the desert floor, contemplating his sins. His moans and groans were the last sounds (hey heard as they walked away. They were already planning the celebration and "Challenge" games they would enjoy without his menacing presence. Seth turned around one last time to see his pet lamb lift his leg over the tyrant's head. The lamb's happy bleating and Seth's famous grin spoke for everyone.

And thus, on the mountain of the Lord it was provided.

Amer-I-can

No ordinary man this fighter, when on his knees he prayed, Five thousand years of tyranny proclaims the tyrants paid!

Dear God, please forgive me and grant this one request, Throw off the yoke of tyranny and put me to Thy test:

Of faith and hope and love, in keeping with your Son. For these great gifts I pledge, my Quiet Revolution

# ABRAHAM, ISAAC AND THE ALTAR OF FIRE

By Joe S. Amer-I-Can

## STUDY GUIDE

### VOCABULARY

Aura
Cadre
Entreaty
Foretell
Gallantry
God
Hebrew
Intimidation
Jaunty
Jesus Christ
Maniacal
Nephilim
Plateau
Precipitous
Pummeling
Revered
Righteous
Sauntered
Speculate
Testimony
The Bible
Vengeance
Vile
Wrath

## Vocabulary Definitions

**Aura: 1.** An invisible breath or emanation. 2. A distinctive air or quality that characterizes a person or thing.

**Cadre: 1.** Framework. 2. A nucleus of trained personnel around which a large organization can be built.

**Entreaty**: An ernest request or petition; plea.

**Foretell:** To tell of or indicate before hand; predict.

**Gallantry:** Nobility of spirit or action; courage.

**God:** A being conceived as the perfect, omnipotent originator and ruler of the universe, the principal object of faith and worship in monotheistic religions.

**Hebrew:** 1. A member or descendant of a northern Semitic people; Israelite.

**Intimidation:** To make timid, threaten.

**Jaunty:** Having a buoyant or self confidant air.

**Jesus Christ:** The founder of Christianity, revered by Christians as the; son of God and the Messiah.

**Maniacal:** Insane; excessive enthusiasm.

**Nephilim:** A Biblical reference to a giant people.

**Plateau:** An elevated and comparatively level expanse of land; tableland.

**Precipitous:** To throw from or as if from a great height; extremely steep.

**Pummeling:** To beat.

**Revered:** To regard with awe, great respect, or devotion.

**Righteous:** Meeting the standards of what is right and just; morally right.

**Righteous:** Meeting the standards of what is right and just; morally right.

**Speculate:** To meditate on a given subject; reflect.

**The Bible:** The sacred book of Judaism (Old Testament) and Christianity (Old and New Testament).

**Testimony:** A declaration or affirmation of fact or truth, as that given before a court.

**Vengeance:** The act or motive of punishing another in payment for a wrong or injury he has committed; retribution.

**Vile:** Loathsome, disgusting.

**Wrath:** Violent, resentful anger; rage; fury. 2. a. a manifestation of anger. B. Divine retribution for sin.

## STUDY QUESTIONS

Why do you think the author wrote this modern day version of an ancient Biblical story?

As demonstrated by the bully Tubal, what can we learn about the concentration of power in the hands of a king, a government or a dictator?

What is the main thing the Hornets did that the Raiders did not do?

What is The Bible? And why is it important to Western Civilization and America?

Why do 92% of Americans believe in God and 85% call themselves Christians? Sadly, these numbers have gone down considerably since this book was written.

What percentage of the ideas of freedom and equal representation for the ordinary person expressed in America's Constitution come from the Bible, and which part of the Bible did most of them come from?

# ABRAHAM, ISAAC AND THE
# ALTAR OF FIRE

**ANSWERS TO STYUDY THE QUESTIONS**

(The following questions and answers contain the views and opinions of the author. They should be researched and verified before being accepted).

*Why do you think the author wrote this modern day version of an ancient Biblical story?*

As a young person, the author had a difficult time understanding how a loving God could ask a father to sacrifice his one and only son. It wasn't until he became a "Born again Christian" that he understood < iod was telling his people he wouldn't ask one of us to do anything he wouldn't do himself. This story is to explain why we are meant to know, love, trust and serve God. God was preparing his people for the future coming of Jesus.

*As demonstrated by the bully, Tubal, what can we learn about the concentration of power in the hands of any form of dictatorship?.*

A famous Christian, British statesman, Lord Acton, wrote: "Power tends to corrupt, and absolute power corrupts absolutely." His statement may be applied to individuals as well as governments. The framers and signers of our Amer-I can Constitution feared they might create (he possibility of a giant, parasitic, central government. Ordinary people had been suffering under the brutality of some form of dictatorship/ royalty for over 5,000 years. This is why America is so exceptional — because (many believe) God blessed a Constitution which allowed us to govern ourselves, with very few and plain laws. It was the first time ever such a government by "We the People" was imagined! (If one of our states wanted to enact laws which were specific to that state, they were free to do so).

Our founders knew that people are prone to take the path of least resistance and become too dependent on a centralized government trying to provide for a dependent people. (The average bureaucrat in Washington today makes $126,000 per year, including free health insurance and other benefits most Amer-I cans cannot attain). Today, one out of every six of us are on some form of government assistance, and a little less than half of us pay for that assistance through our federal income taxes. The rest not only do not pay any federal income tax, but receive thousands of dollars from our federal government in what are unfairly referred to as "Earned Income Tax Credits"!

This welfare state mentality in one of the main reasons our Congress is unable to balance our budget and why we are $16 trillion dollars in debt. (Now almost 32 trillion in debt!)

Many of our founders also feared the concept of a "Central Bank," where money can be printed (now digitized) without the consent of Congress, which causes inflation and the cheapening of the Amer-I can dollar. When there is an abundance of dollars for "Everyone" the value of the dollar goes down. Consider this extreme example: If everyone were a millionaire, how much money would a truly rich person have to have?

(Answer: It's not possible to print/digitize that much money. Trying to do so will eventually destroy our free enterprise system and America)! Trying desperately to provide for everyone leads to socialism, where power is concentrated in the hands of an elite few (bullies). Once a republic loses the value of its currency, free enterprise is defeated and socialism reigns.

*What did the Hornets do that the Raiders did not do?*

Like America's founders and framers, they prayed to the God of The Bible.

*What is the importance of The Bible to Western Civilization and America?*

Their Bibles were the most prized possessions of a small group of European Christians who boarded the Mayflower and prayed their way across rough seas to America's shores in the early 1600's. (If your family felt like they had to go to the moon in order to be free, would you pray about that trip)? Our early Christian escapees of oppression were the first of what was to be nearly two million Amer-I can Christian founders who would fight for their independence from the King of England. The guys with the suspenders, worn britches and squir rel rifles would defeat the guys with the bright red uniforms and the greatest army and navy in the world! (I low does this happen without prayer)? It was also their private and public devotion and prayers Io (he God of the Bible which enabled them to envision a country which would honor the beliefs of all individuals by not forcing their ( hristian beliefs on anyone.

However, John Adams, our second president, said, "()ur ('onstilu tion was made for a moral and religious people; it is wholly inadequate to the government of any other." 'Hie author of "Abraham, Isaac and the Altar of Fire" believes this means Amer-I cans should be free to worship the highest moral standard (God), or our government wdl eventually require standards that do away with the God of the Bible.

Today our government no longer defends marriage as between one man and one woman. When the author was young in the 1960's, divorce was so unusual it was considered by some to be as scandalous as a child born out of wedlock (marriage). Today, even in small cities and towns, both circumstances are more common than what used to be and are considered the "New normal"!

Until the early 1960's, God's history with America was taught and respected in our public schools. Prayer was not only allowed there, but encouraged. When America's children recited our Pledge ol Al legiance and the phrase, "One nation under (iod," they knew they weir also pledging to the God of The Bible. Today, because oui Icderal government has removed prayer and devotion to (>od from oui public classrooms, many of nearly three generations of American i liihlim me ignorant of our Judeo Christian history.

Some early Americans called John Adams sanctimonious (loo holy) for his statement about our Constitution I )o you think lie may have been right?

*Why do over 90% of Amer-I cans believe in God and over 80% call themselves Christians?*

America has a Judeo Christian heritage, which means our founders and framers were Christians who believed in the Old and New Testament, but they didn't force their religious beliefs on an entire country. They relied on their own hard work and their belief in The Bible and God. Our thirteen original colonies (later states) were founded by various branches of Christianity. Some of their original state Constitutions required that office holders be Christian.

They were jealous of each others denominations of Christianity. They were about to give up on forming a federal government/ United States (some of the delegates had already given up and gone home), when Benjamin Franklin called for a time of prayer to the God they all believed in. Shortly after those prayers were made to God, they were able to agree on our Constitution.

Today, the author of "Abraham, Isaac and the Altar of Fire" believes our federal government has become like Tubal, only in a disguised manner. By slowly allowing the destruction of our free enterprise economy, our government is forcing millions of Americans to accept government assistance in order to survive. America has lost over ten million manufacturing jobs in the last ten years! Our country will soon be over 35 trillion dollars in debt! Several of our largest corporations pay zero income tax.

*What percentage of the ideas of freedom and free enterprise for the ordinary person expressed in America's Constitution come from The Bible, and which part of The Bible did most of them come from?*

A little over thirty per cent, mostly from the Old Testament book of Deuteronomy. During the Revolutionary War, some Amer-I can pastors actually led members of their congregations in battle against the tyranny of King George of England. King George was the Tubal of his day and age, and the early Amer-I can's who defeated him were the Hornets.

Today, our Tubal is our giant, parasitic federal government; it remains to be seen who the modern day Amer-I can Hornets will be